FINGER GUITAR STYLE NOTES & TAB

kids' favorites

Arranged by Marcel Robinson

ISBN 0-634-04298-X

HAL•LEONARD®
CORPORATION
7777 W. BLUEMOUND RD. P.O. BOX 13819 MILWAUKEE, WI 53213

Visit Hal Leonard Online at
www.halleonard.com

CONTENTS

kids' favorites

Alphabet Song

Traditional

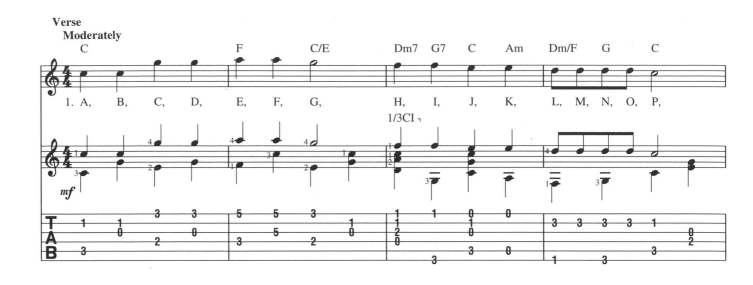

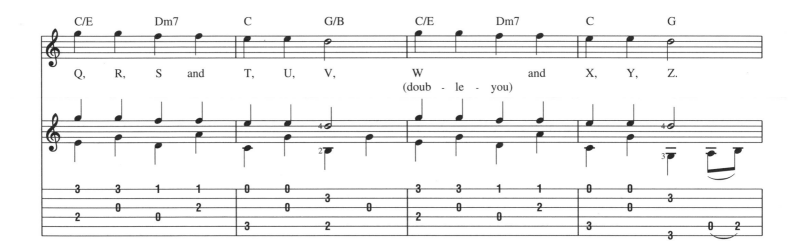

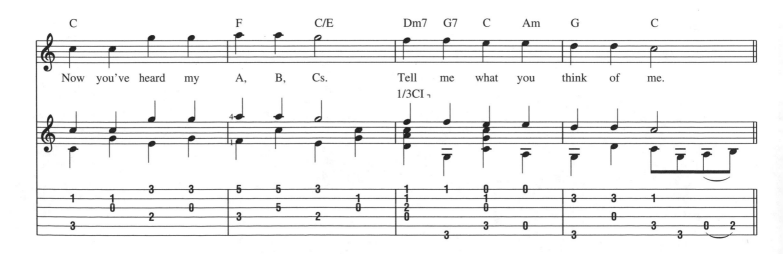

Baa Baa Black Sheep

Traditional

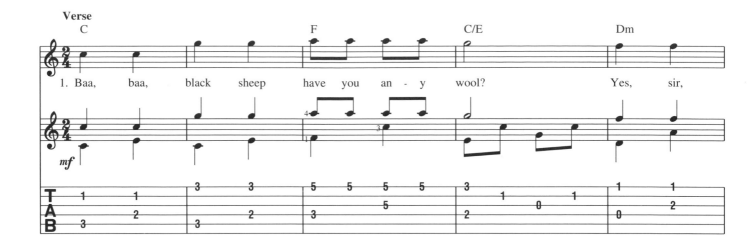

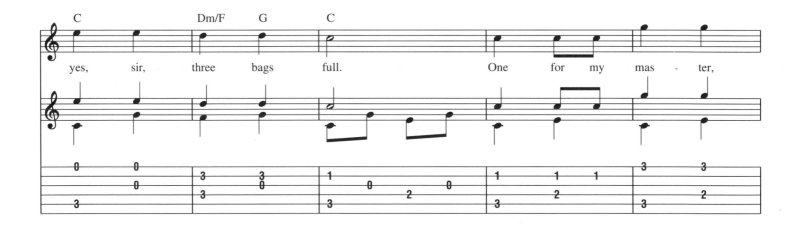

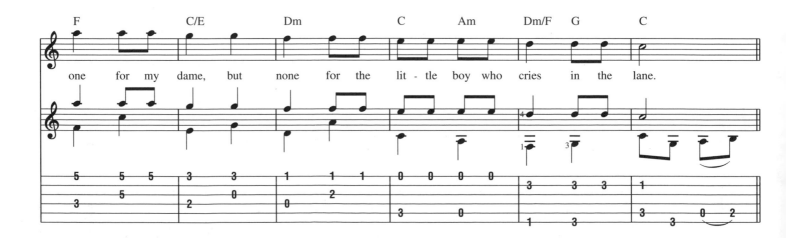

2. Baa, baa, black sheep have you an - y wool? Yes, sir,

yes, sir, three bags full. One for my mas - ter,

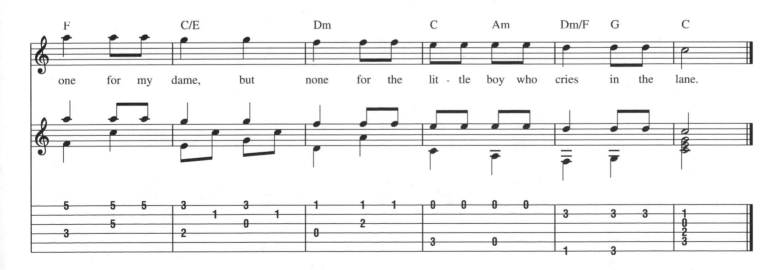

one for my dame, but none for the lit - tle boy who cries in the lane.

Eensy Weensy Spider

Traditional

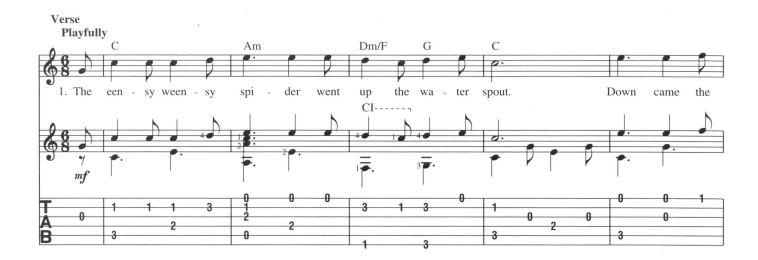

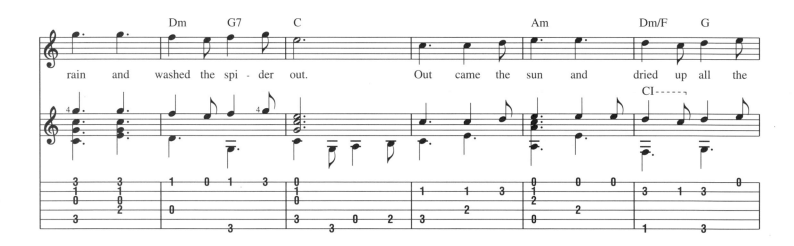

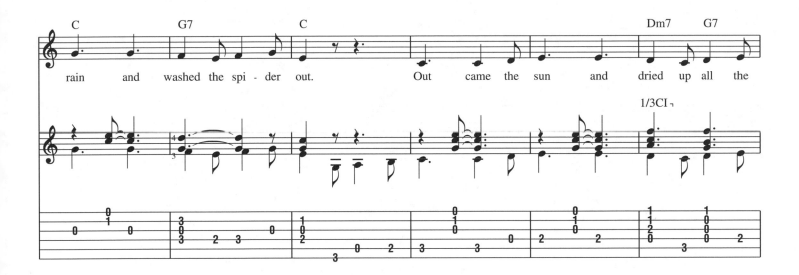

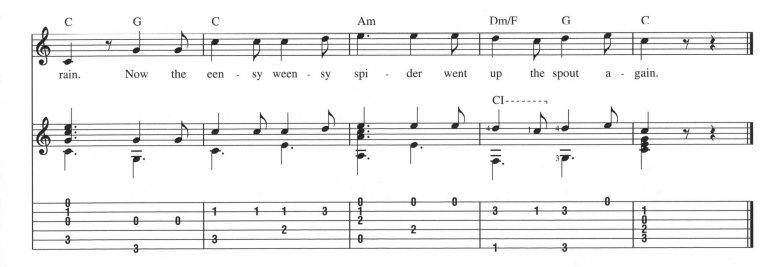

The Farmer in the Dell

Traditional

Drop D tuning:
(low to high) D–A–D–G–B–E

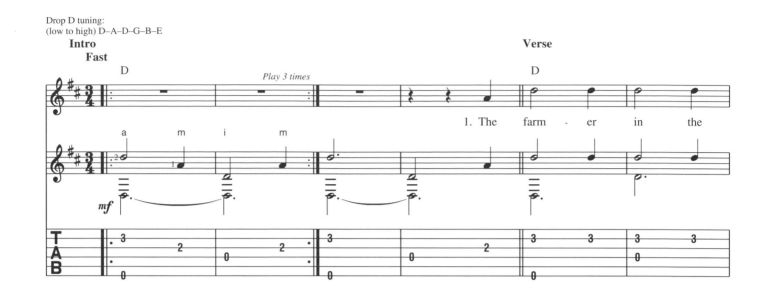

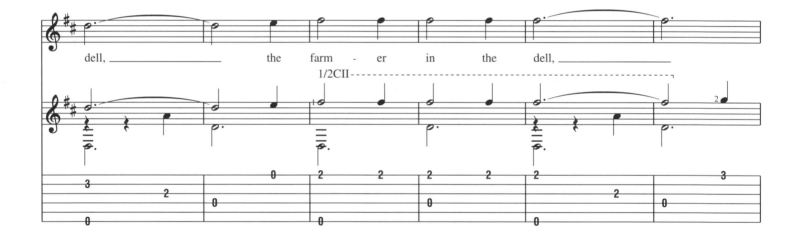

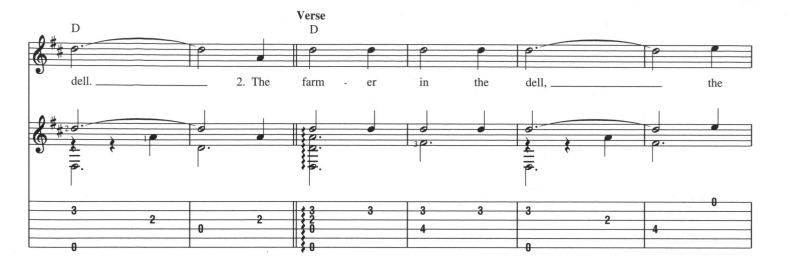

dell. _____ 2. The farm - er in the dell, _____ the

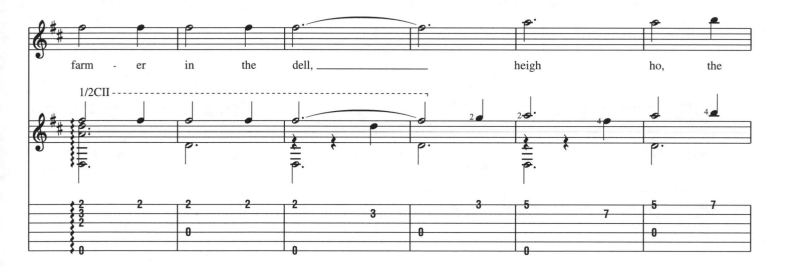

farm - er in the dell, _____ heigh ho, the

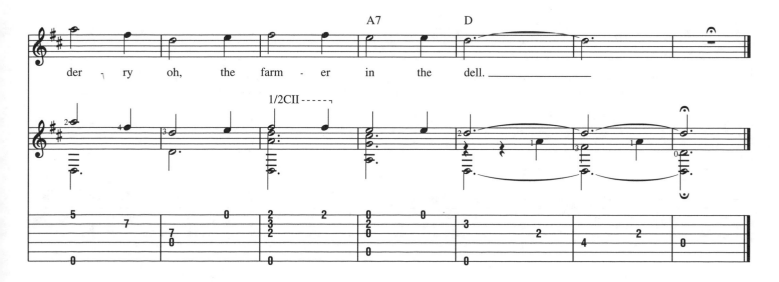

der ry oh, the farm - er in the dell. _____

Frère Jacques
(Are You Sleeping?)

Traditional

Drop D tuning:
(low to high) D–A–D–G–B–E

Verse
Moderately

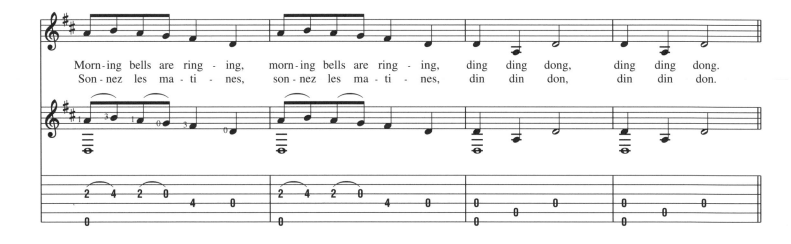

English: 1. Are you sleep-ing, are you sleep-ing, broth-er John, broth-er John?
French: 1. Frè-re Jac-ques, Frè-re Jac-ques, dor-mez vous, dor-mez vous?

Morn-ing bells are ring-ing, morn-ing bells are ring-ing, ding ding dong, ding ding dong.
Son-nez les ma-ti-nes, son-nez les ma-ti-nes, din din don, din din don.

Verse

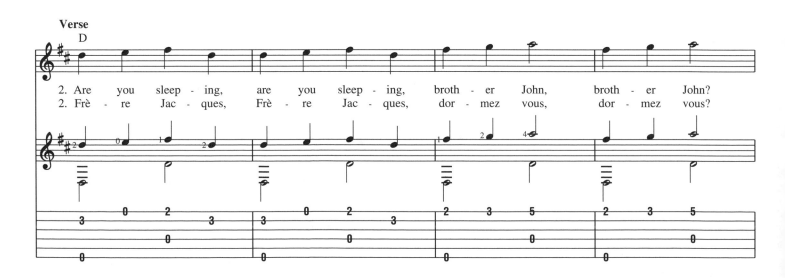

2. Are you sleep-ing, are you sleep-ing, broth-er John, broth-er John?
2. Frè-re Jac-ques, Frè-re Jac-ques, dor-mez vous, dor-mez vous?

Morn-ing bells are ring - ing, morn-ing bells are ring - ing, ding ding dong, ding ding dong.
Son - nez les ma - ti - nes, son - nez les ma - ti - nes, din din don, din din don.

Round

Hickory Dickory Dock

Traditional

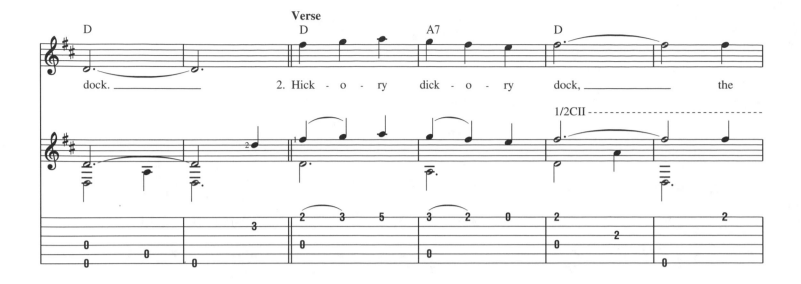

dock. _____ 2. Hick - o - ry dick - o - ry dock, _____ the

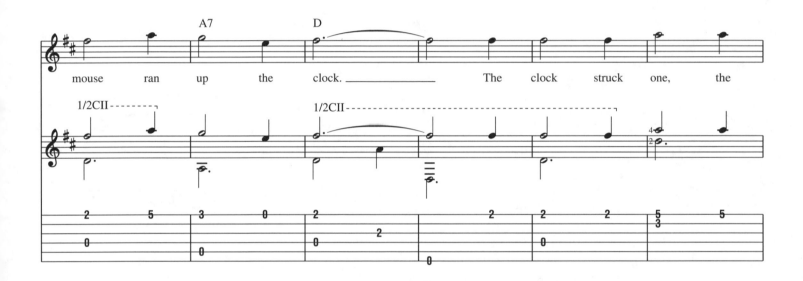

mouse ran up the clock. _____ The clock struck one, the

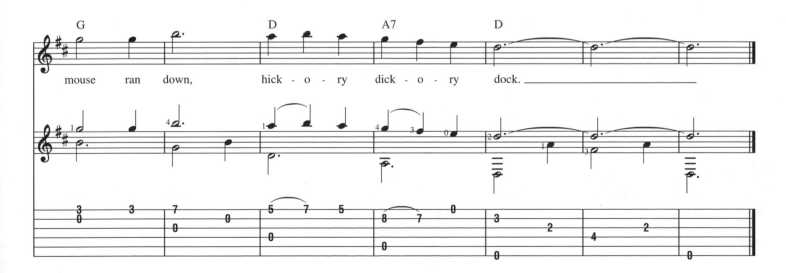

mouse ran down, hick - o - ry dick - o - ry dock. _____

Humpty Dumpty

Traditional

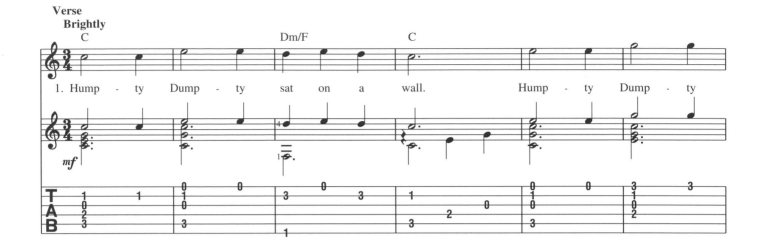

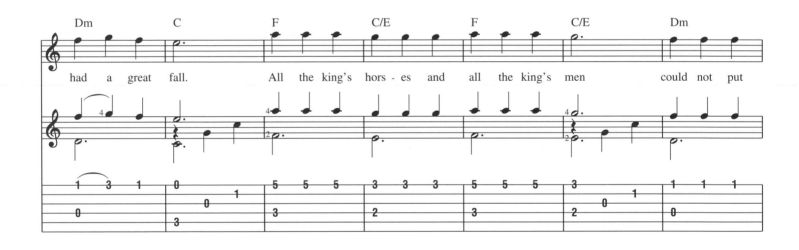

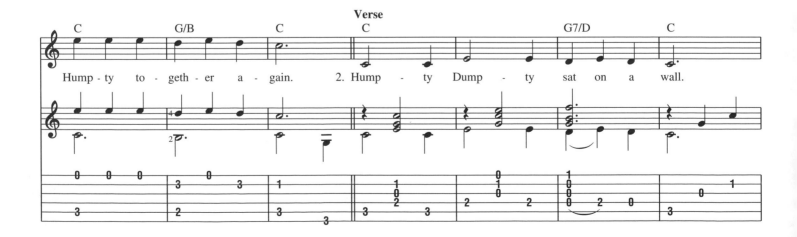

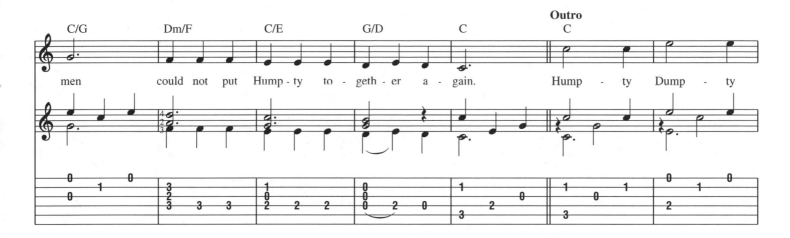

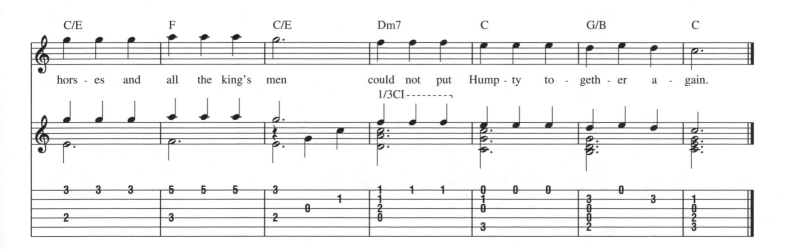

I've Been Working on the Railroad

Traditional American Folksong

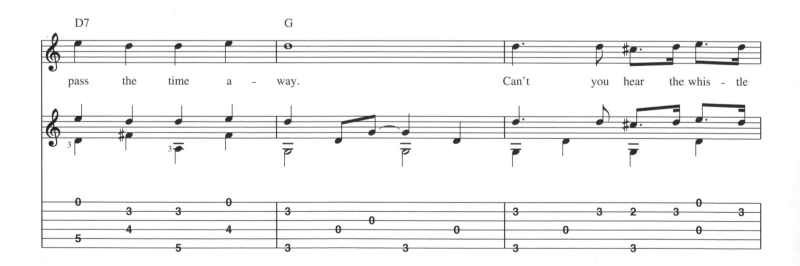

blow - in'? ___ Rise up so ear - ly in the morn'.

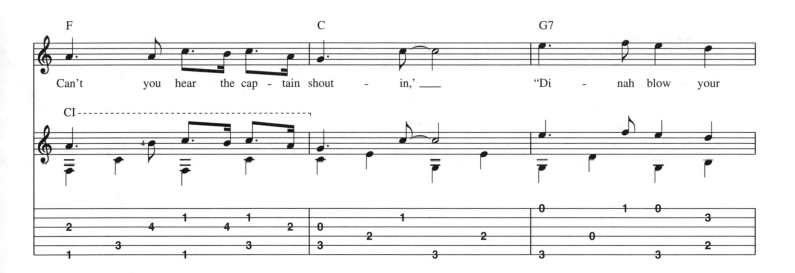

Can't you hear the cap - tain shout - in,' ___ "Di - nah blow your

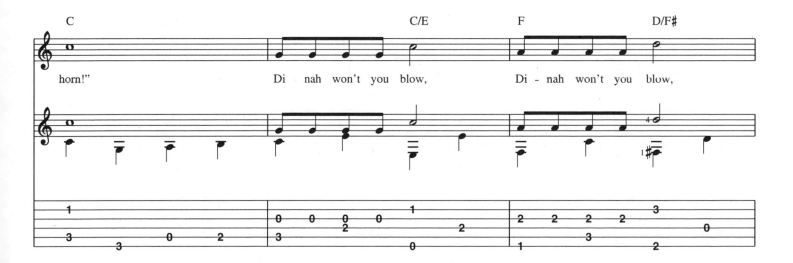

horn!" Di - nah won't you blow, Di - nah won't you blow,

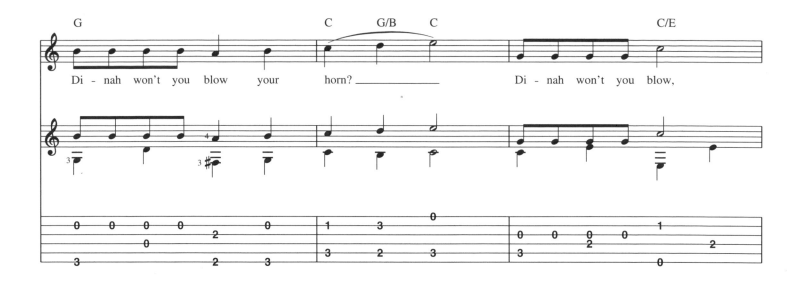

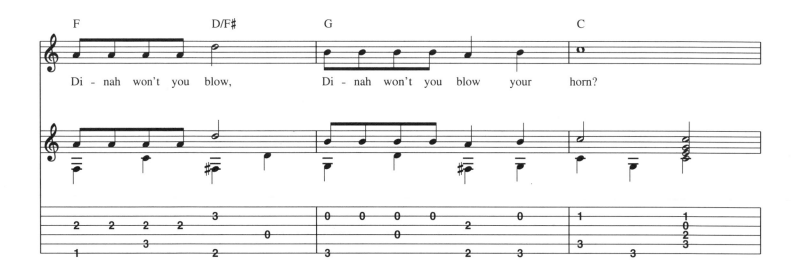

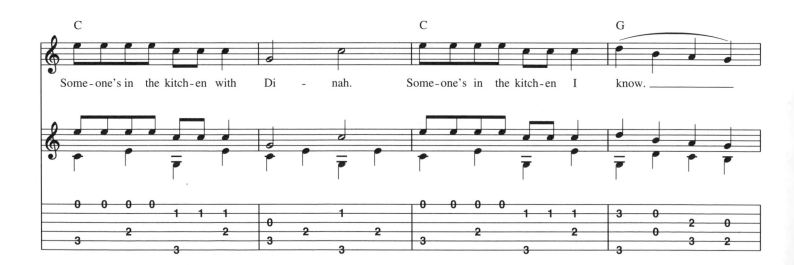

Some-one's in the kitch-en with Di - nah, strum-min' on the old ban - jo and sing-in',

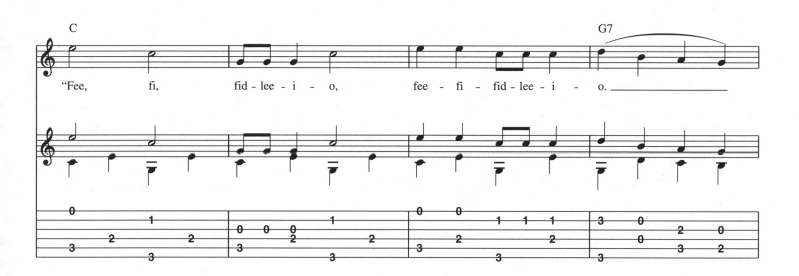

"Fee, fi, fid-lee - i - o, fee - fi - fid-lee - i - o. _____

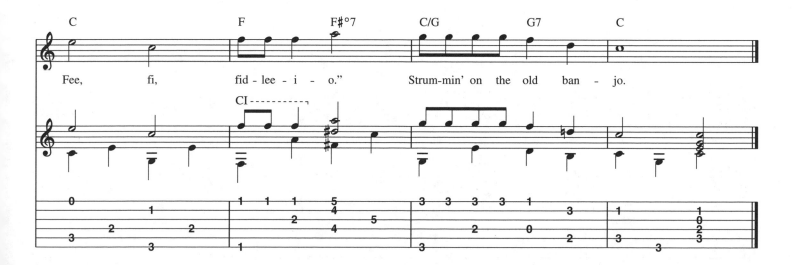

Fee, fi, fid-lee - i - o." Strum-min' on the old ban - jo.

It's Raining, It's Pouring

Traditional

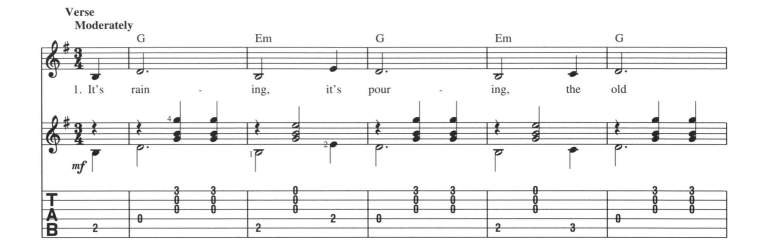

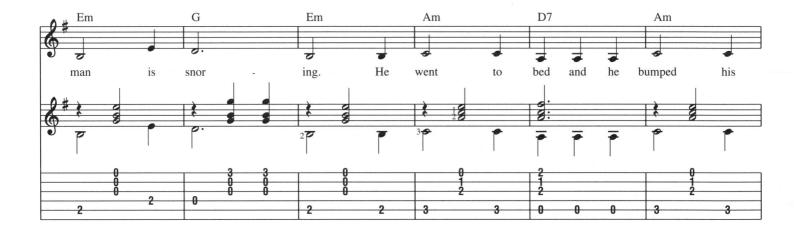

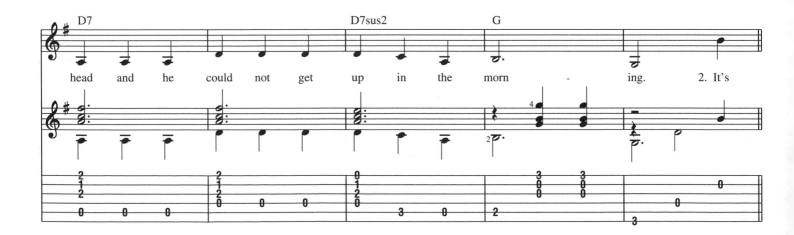

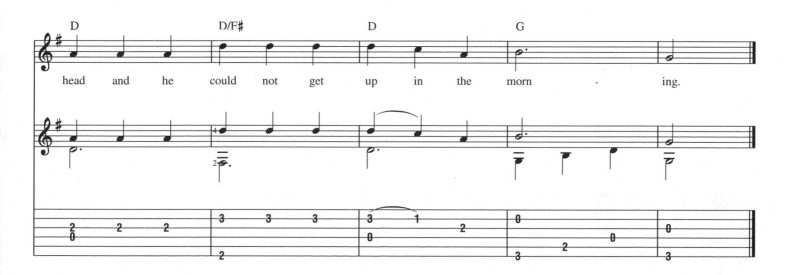

Jesus Loves Me

Words by Anna B. Warner
Music by William B. Bradbury

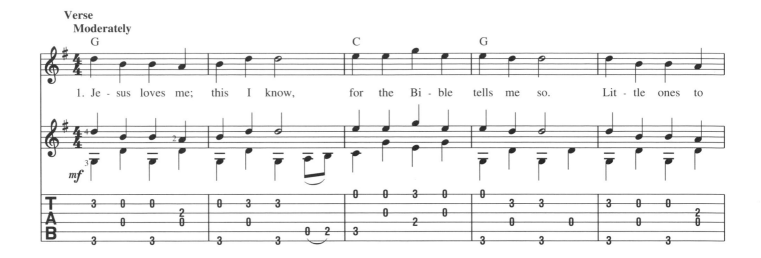

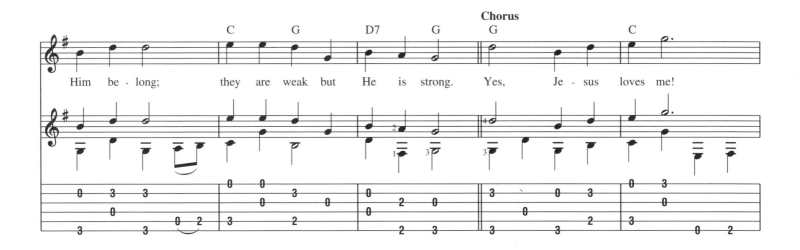

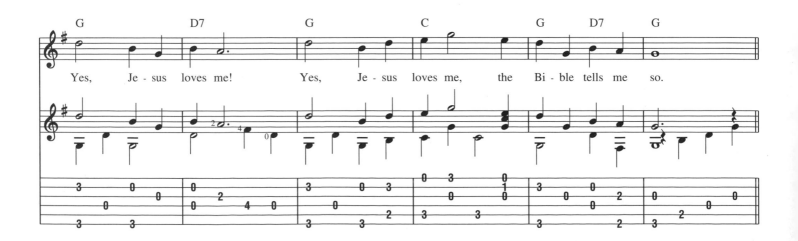

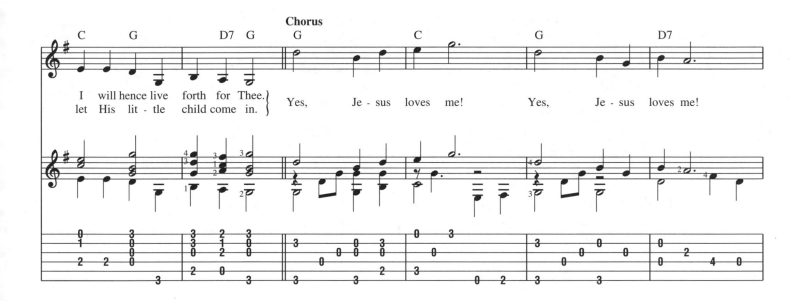

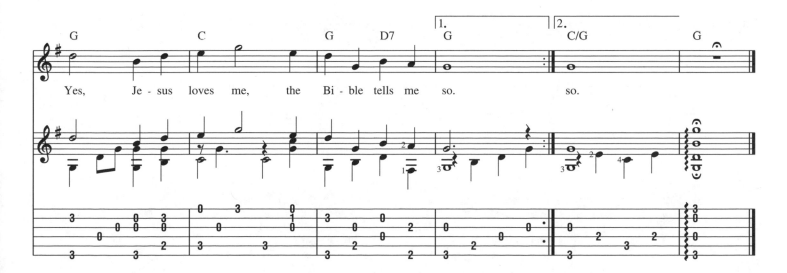

London Bridge

Traditional

London Bridge is falling down, falling down, falling down. London Bridge is

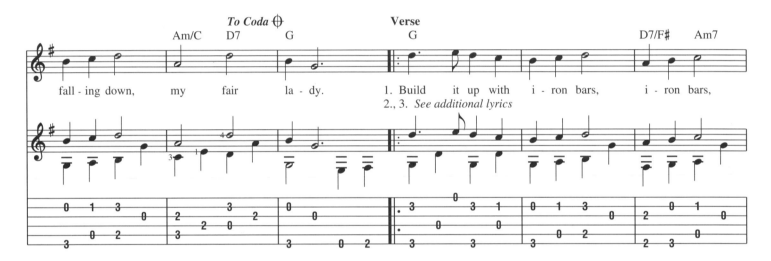

falling down, my fair lady. 1. Build it up with iron bars, iron bars,

2., 3. *See additional lyrics*

 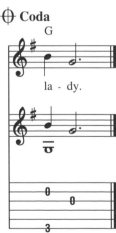

iron bars. Build it up with iron bars, my fair lady. lady.

Additional Lyrics

2. Iron bars will bend and break,
Bend and break, bend and break.
Iron bars will bend and break,
My fair lady.

3. Build it up with gold and silver,
Gold and silver, gold and silver.
Build it up with gold and silver,
My fair lady.

Mary Had a Little Lamb

Words by Sarah Josepha Hale
Traditional Music

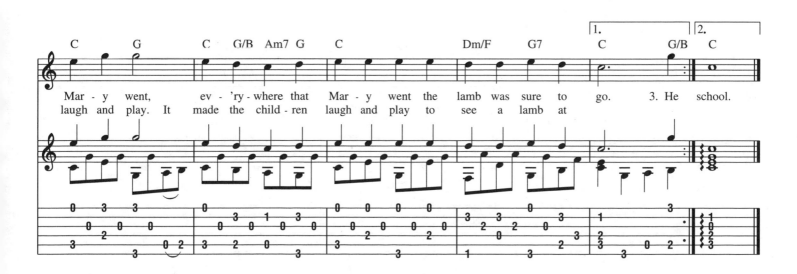

Lullaby
(Cradle Song)

By Johannes Brahms

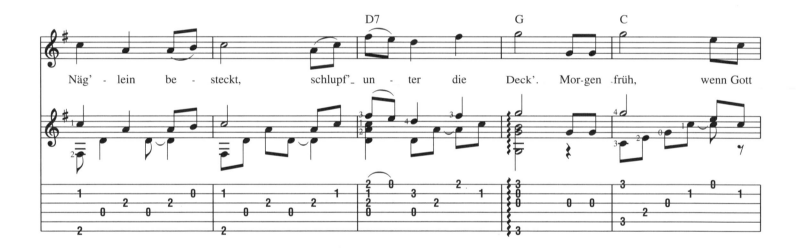

wie - der ge - weckt. 2. Gu - ten a - bend, gut' Nacht, mit __ Ro - sen __ be -

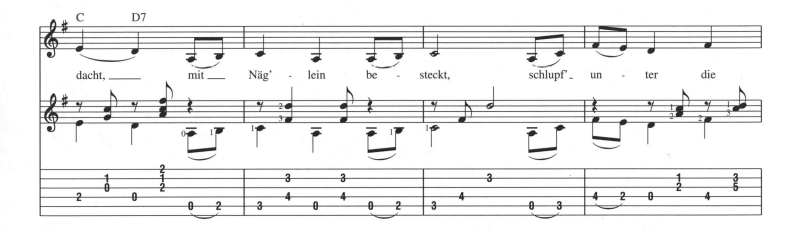

dacht, __ mit __ Näg' - lein be - steckt, schlupf' un - ter die

Deck'. Mor - gen früh, wenn Gott will, wirst du wie - der ge - weckt, mor - gen

früh, wenn Gott will, wirst du wie - der ge - weckt.

The Muffin Man

Traditional

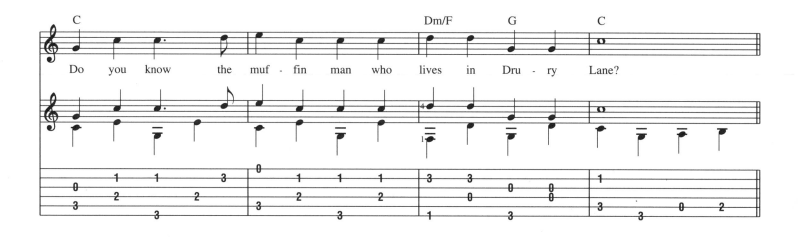

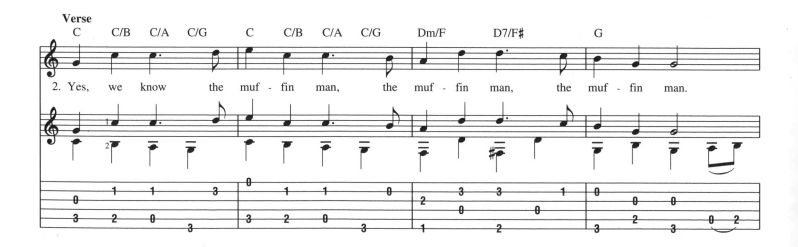

The Mulberry Bush

Traditional

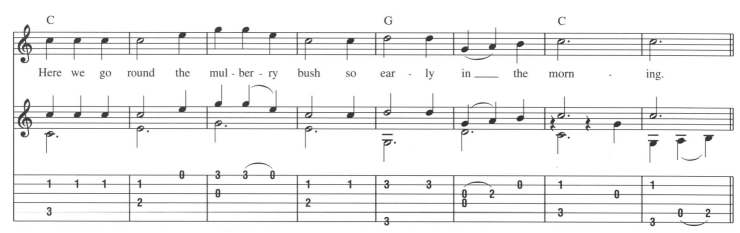

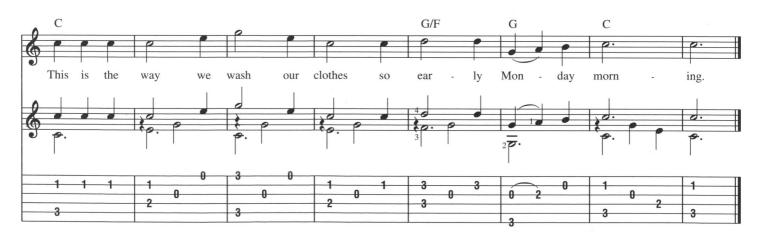

Old MacDonald

Traditional Children's Song

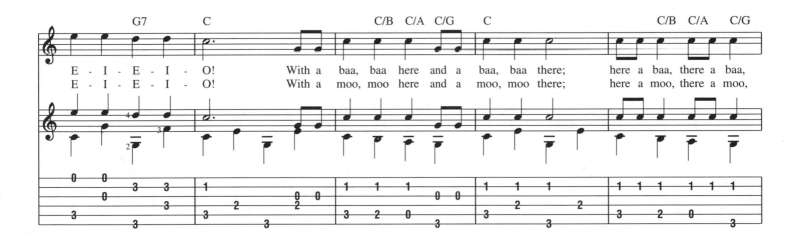

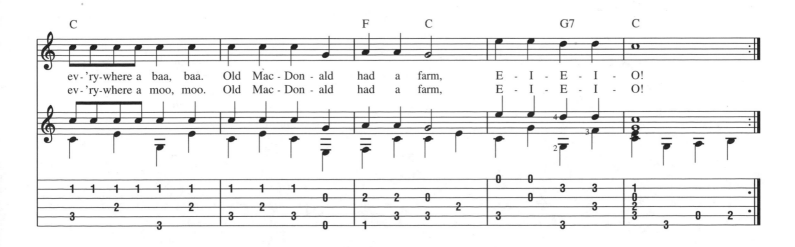

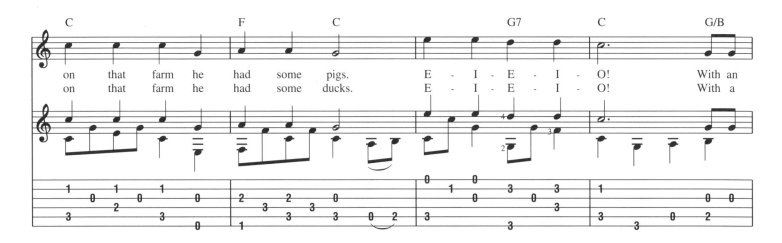

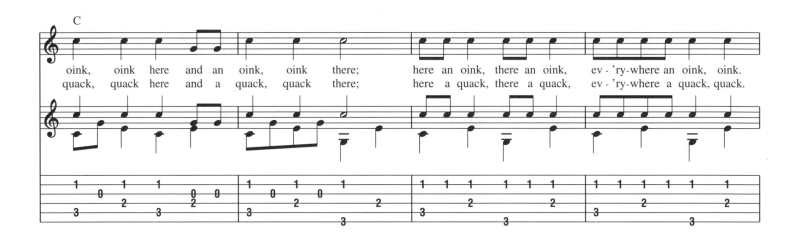

Verse

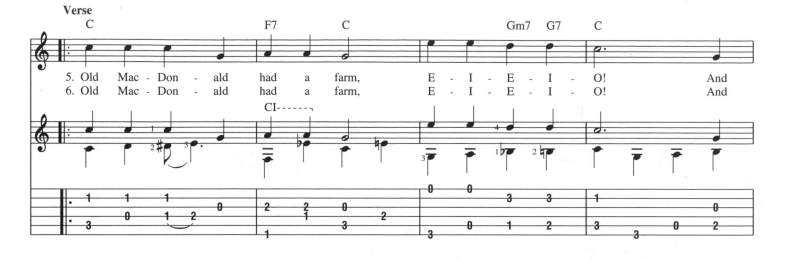

5. Old Mac - Don - ald had a farm, E - I - E - I - O! And
6. Old Mac - Don - ald had a farm, E - I - E - I - O! And

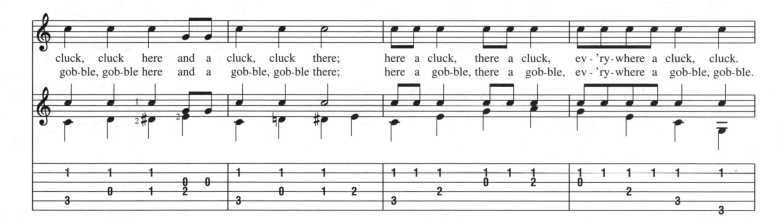

on that farm he had some chick ens. E - I - E - I - O! With a
on that farm he had some tur keys. E - I - E - I - O! With a

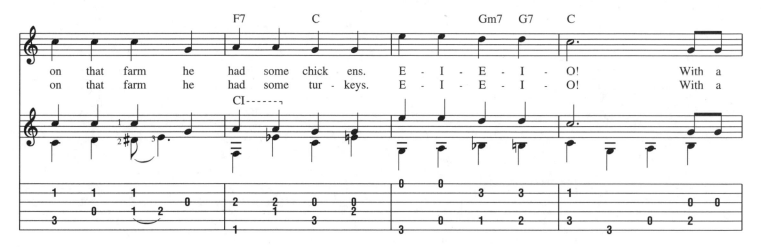

cluck, cluck here and a cluck, cluck there; here a cluck, there a cluck, ev - 'ry-where a cluck, cluck.
gob-ble, gob-ble here and a gob-ble, gob-ble there; here a gob-ble, there a gob-ble, ev - 'ry-where a gob-ble, gob-ble.

Old Mac - Don - ald had a farm, E - I - E - I - O! O!
Old Mac - Don - ald had a farm, E - I - E - I -

Oh! Susanna

Words and Music by Stephen Collins Foster

san - na, _____ oh, don't you cry for me, _____ for I

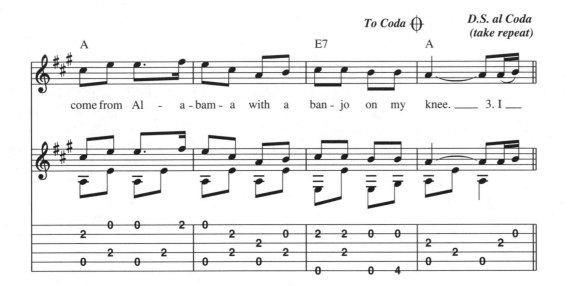

come from Al - a - bam - a with a ban - jo on my knee. ___ 3. I ___

know.

Additional Lyrics

3. I had a dream the other night
   When everything was still.
   I thought I saw Susanna
   A-coming down the hill.

4. The buckwheat cake was in her mouth
   The tear was in her eye.
   Say I, "I'm coming from the South,
   Susanna, don't you cry."

Oh Where, Oh Where
Has My Little Dog Gone

Words by Sep. Winner
Traditional Melody

1. Oh where, oh where has my lit-tle dog gone? Oh where, oh

where can he be? _____ With his hair so short and his

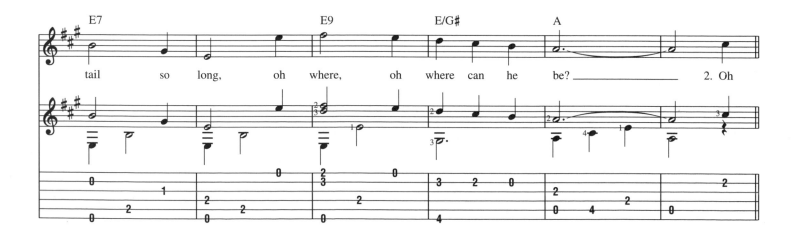

tail so long, oh where, oh where can he be? _____ 2. Oh

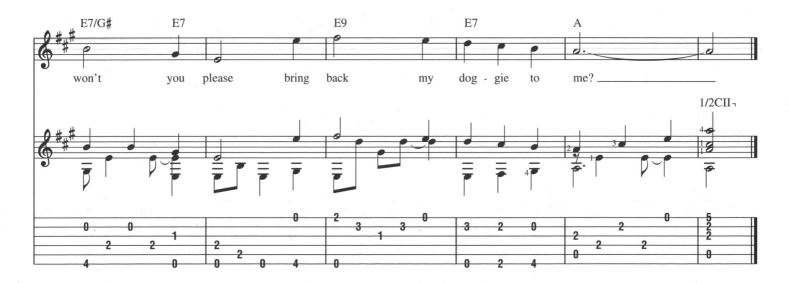

On Top of Old Smoky

Traditional

Additional Lyrics

2. Well, a-courting's a pleasure,
   And parting is grief.
   But a false hearted lover
   Is worse than a thief.

3. A thief, he will rob you
   And take all you have,
   But a false-hearted lover
   Will send you to your grave.

6. They'll tell you they love you,
   Just to give your heart ease.
   But the minute your back's turned,
   They'll court whom they please.

4. And the grave will decay you
   And turn you to dust.
   And where is the young man
   A poor girl can trust?

7. So come all you young maidens
   And listen to me.
   Never place your affection
   On a green willow tree.

5. They'll hug you and kiss you
   And tell you more lies
   Than the cross-ties on the railroad,
   Or the stars in the skies.

8. For the leaves they will whither
   And the roots they will die.
   And your true love will leave you,
   And you'll never know why.

Polly Wolly Doodle

Traditional American Minstrel Song

fay. For I'm goin' to Lou' - si - an - a for to see my Sus - y - an - na sing - ing

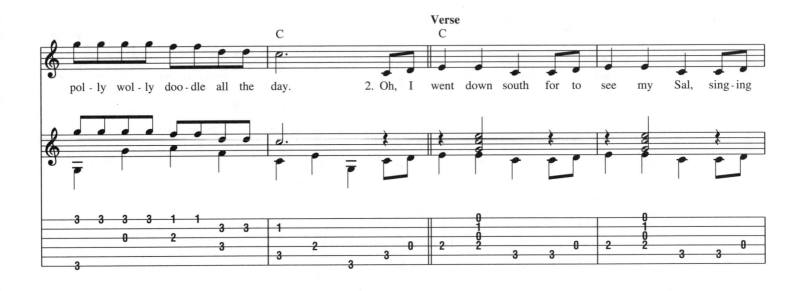

pol - ly wol - ly doo - dle all the day. 2. Oh, I went down south for to see my Sal, sing - ing

pol - ly wol - ly doo - dle all the day. My _ Sal - ly is a _ spunk - y gal, sing

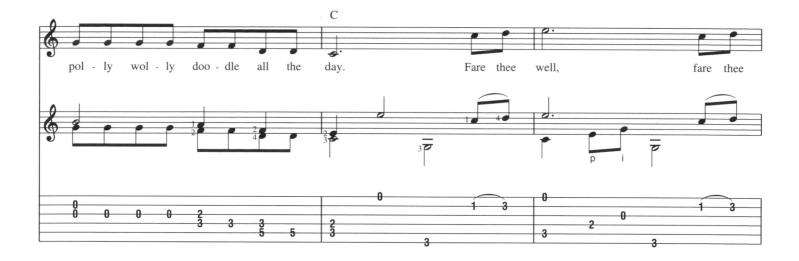

pol - ly wol - ly doo - dle all the day. Fare thee well, fare thee

well, fare thee well, my fair - y fay. For I'm goin' to Lou' - si - an - a for to

see my Sus - y - an - na sing - ing pol - ly wol - ly doo - dle all the day.

Ring Around the Rosie

Traditional

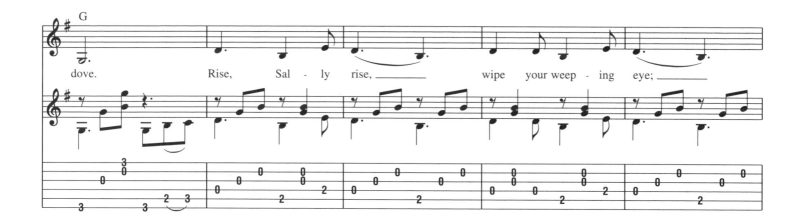

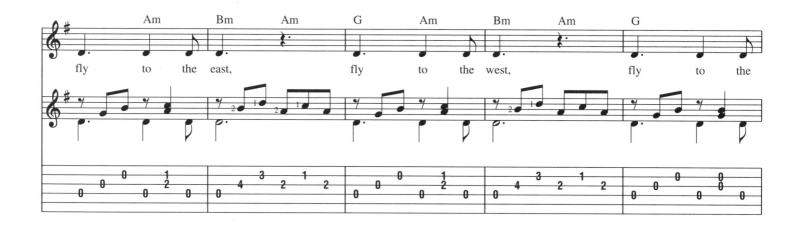

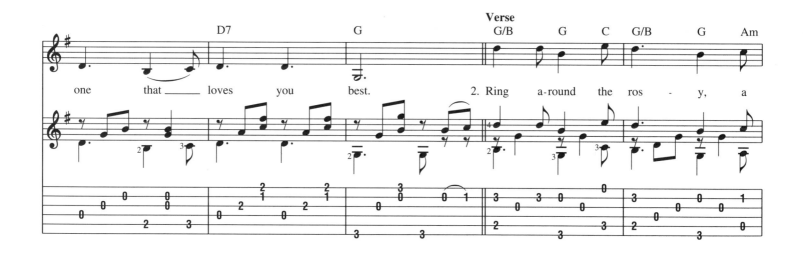

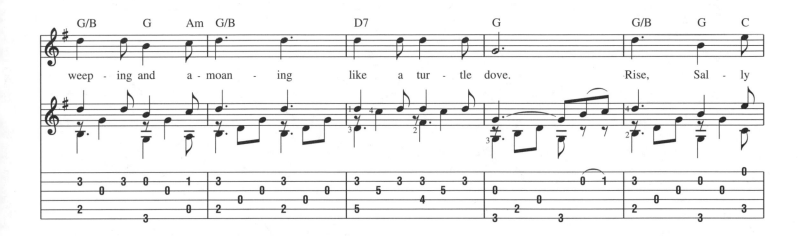

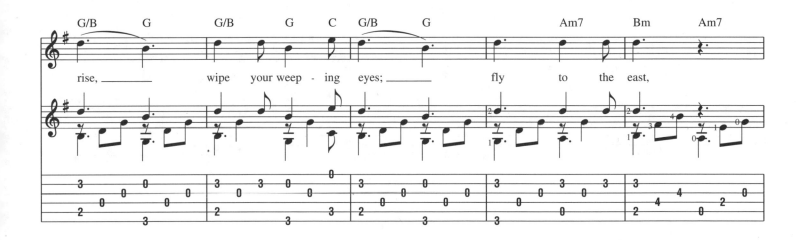

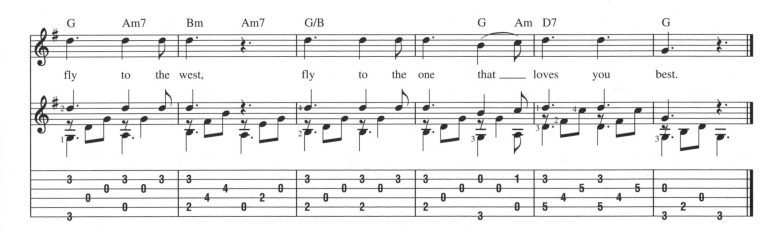

Pop Goes the Weasel

Traditional

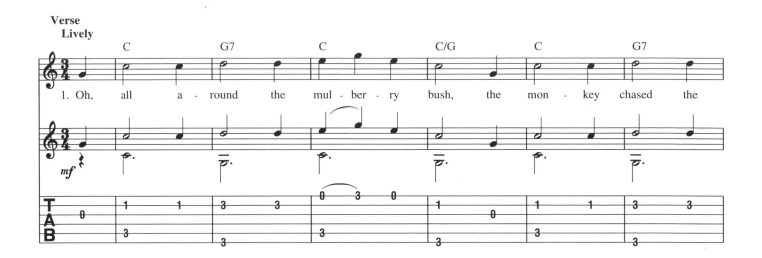

1. Oh, all a - round the mul - ber - ry bush, the mon - key chased the

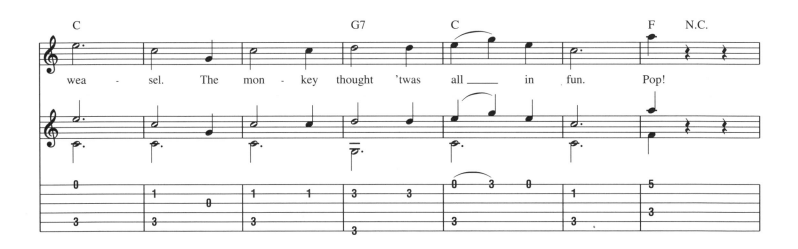

wea - sel. The mon - key thought 'twas all ___ in fun. Pop!

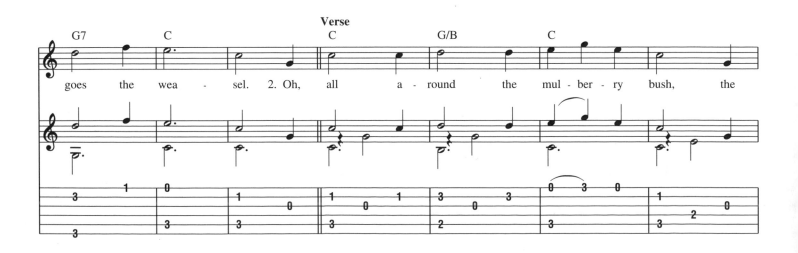

goes the wea - sel. 2. Oh, all a - round the mul - ber - ry bush, the

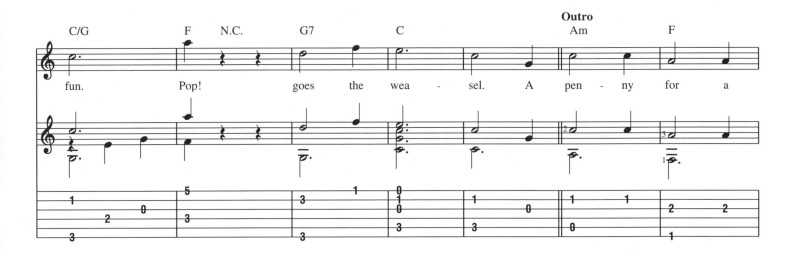

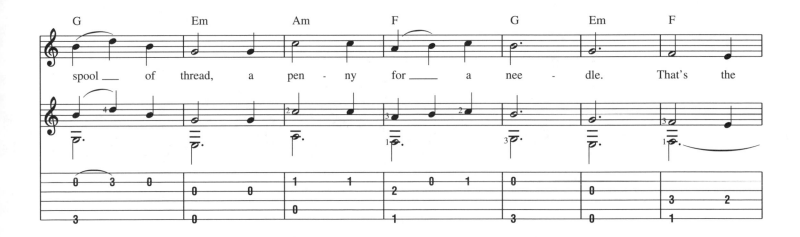

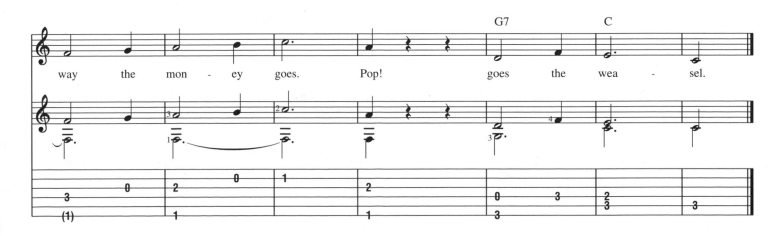

Rock-A-Bye, Baby

Traditional

Drop D tuning:
(low to high) D–A–D–G–B–E

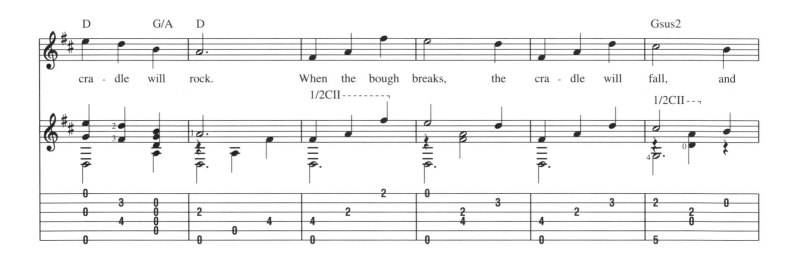

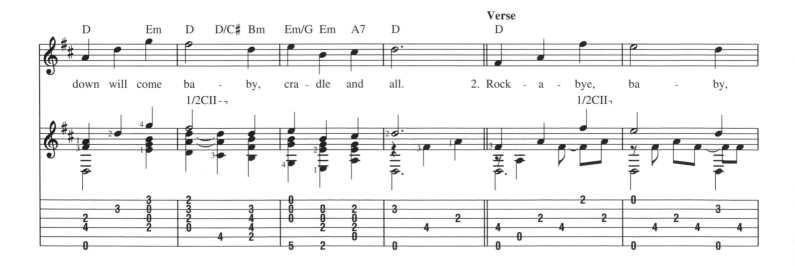

on the tree top, when the wind blows, the cra - dle will

rock. When the bough breaks, the cra - dle will fall, and

down will come ba - by, cra - dle and all.

Row, Row, Row Your Boat

Traditional

Drop D tuning:
(low to high) D–A–D–G–B–E

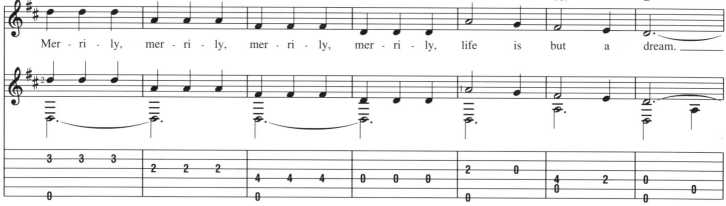

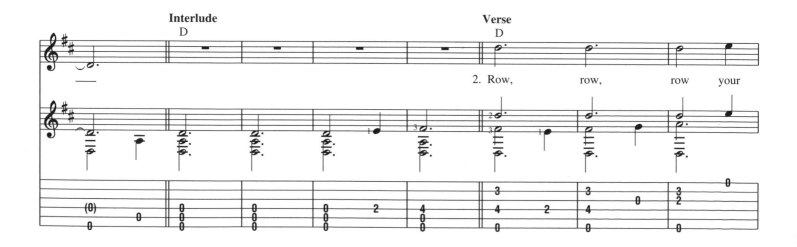

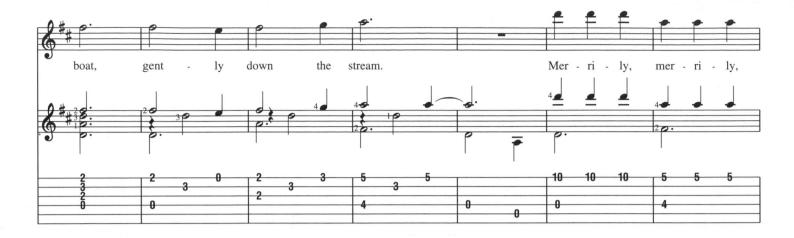

boat, gent - ly down the stream. Mer - ri - ly, mer - ri - ly,

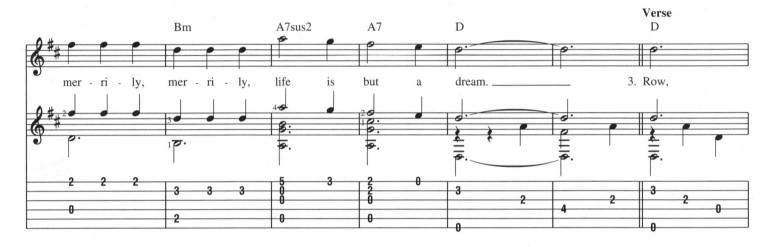

Verse

Bm　A7sus2　A7　D　D

mer - ri - ly, mer - ri - ly, life is but a dream. _____ 3. Row,

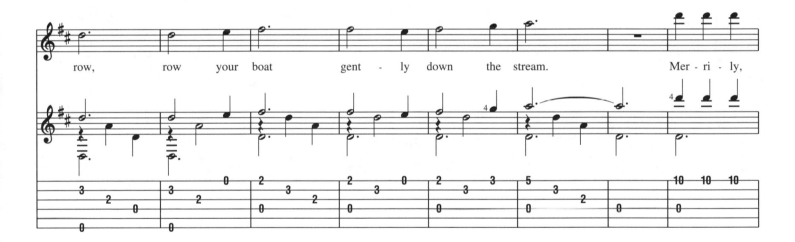

row, row your boat gent - ly down the stream. Mer - ri - ly,

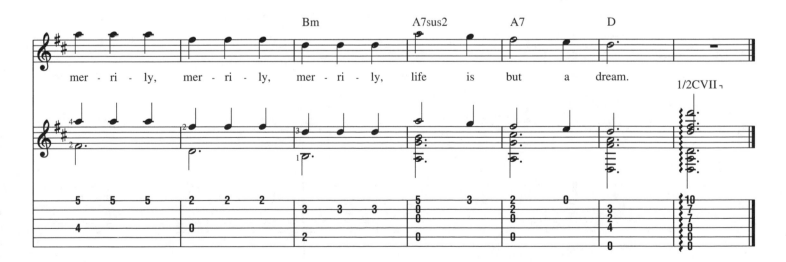

Bm　A7sus2　A7　D

mer - ri - ly, mer - ri - ly, mer - ri - ly, life is but a dream.

1/2CVII

Sailing, Sailing

Words and Music by Godfrey Marks

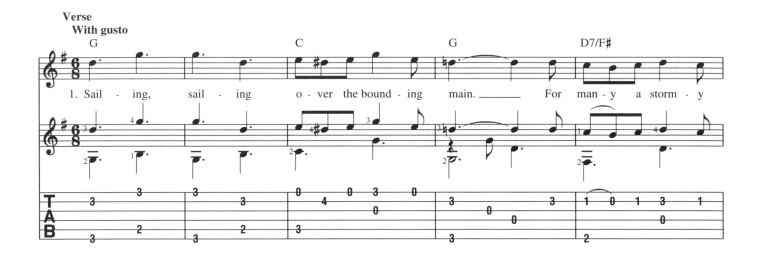

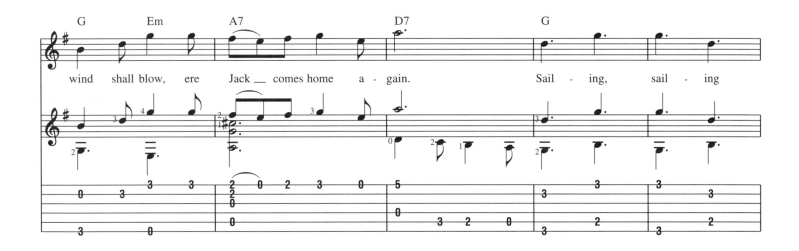

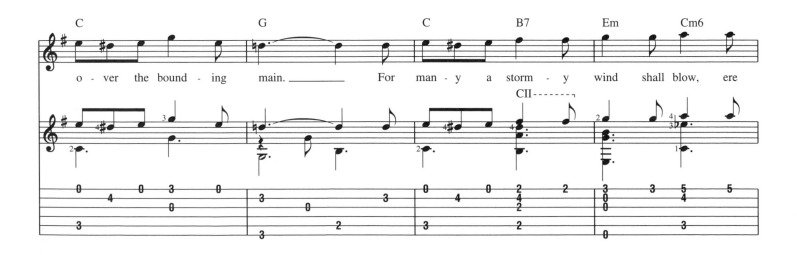

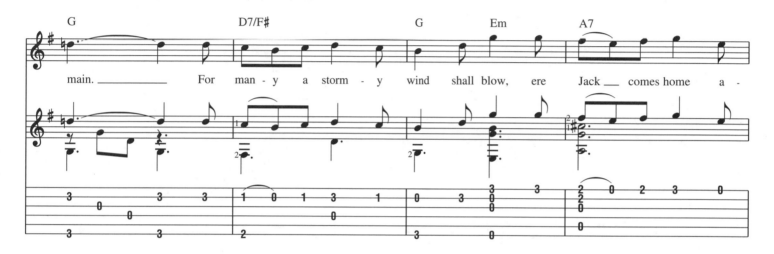

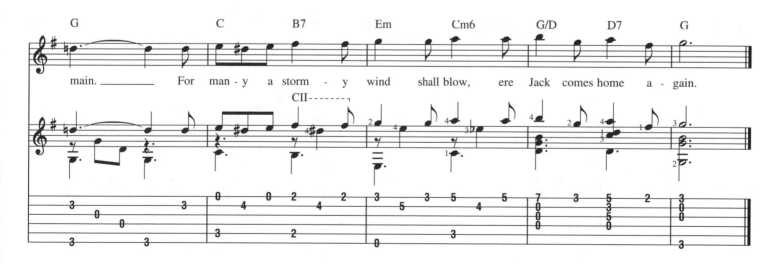

Sing a Song of Sixpence

Traditional

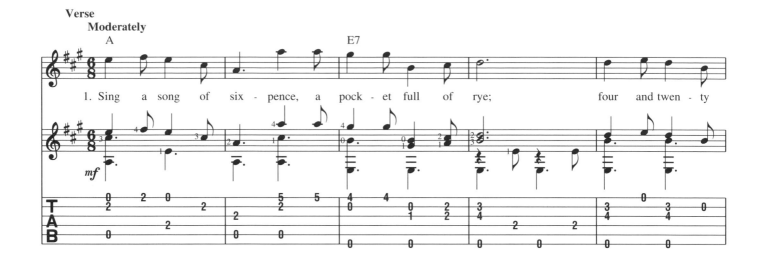

1. Sing a song of six - pence, a pock - et full of rye; four and twen - ty

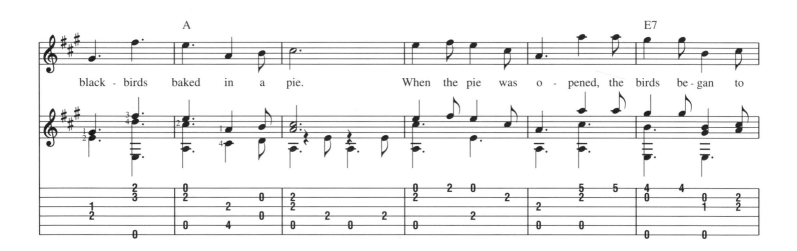

black - birds baked in a pie. When the pie was o - pened, the birds be - gan to

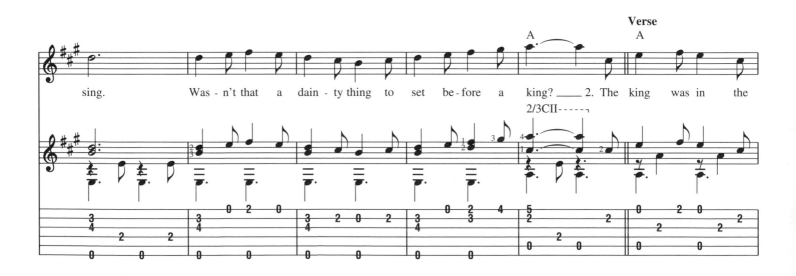

sing. Was - n't that a dain - ty thing to set be - fore a king? ___ 2. The king was in the

count - ing house, count - ing all his mon - ey. _____ The queen was in the par - lor,

eat - ing bread and hon - ey. _____ The maid was in the gar - den, hang - ing out the

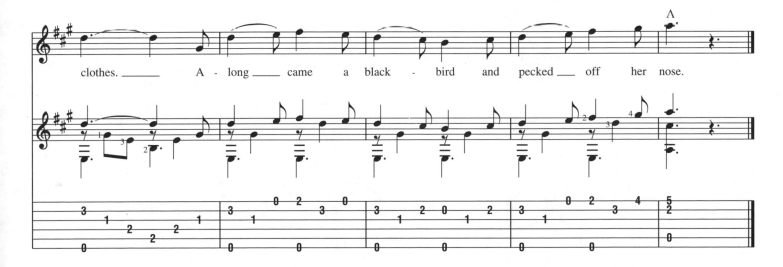

clothes. _____ A - long _____ came a black - bird and pecked _____ off her nose.

Skip to My Lou

Traditional

1. Choose your part - ners, skip to my lou, choose your part - ners, skip to my lou,

choose your part - ners, skip to my lou, skip to my lou, my dar - ling.

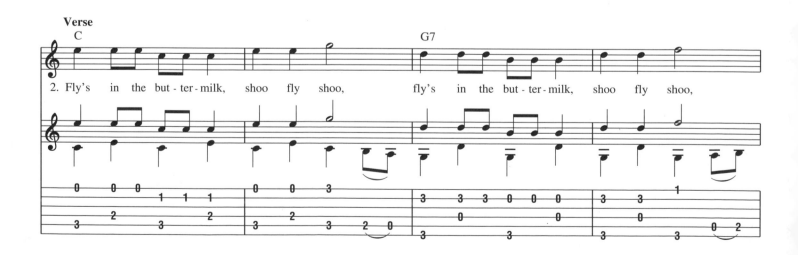

2. Fly's in the but - ter - milk, shoo fly shoo, fly's in the but - ter - milk, shoo fly shoo,

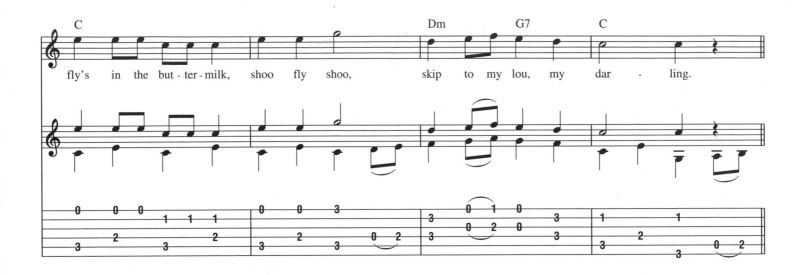

fly's in the but-ter-milk, shoo fly shoo, skip to my lou, my dar - ling.

Verse

3. Choose your part - ners, skip to my lou, choose your part - ners, skip to my lou,

choose your part - ners, skip to my lou, skip to my lou, my dar - ling.

This Old Man

Traditional

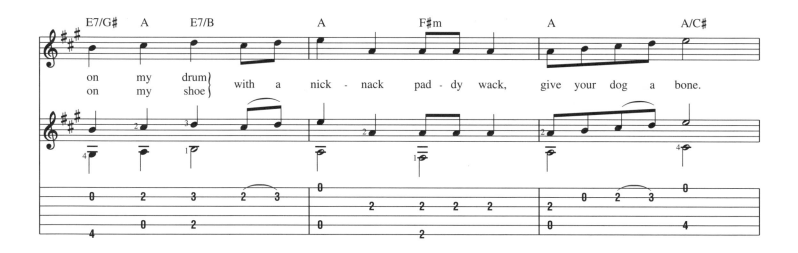

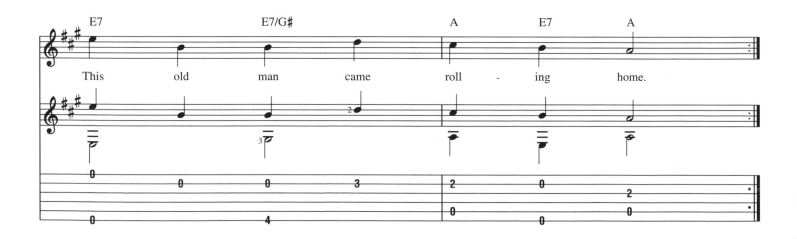

Verse

3. This old man, he played three. He played nick - nack
4. This old man, he played four. He played nick - nack

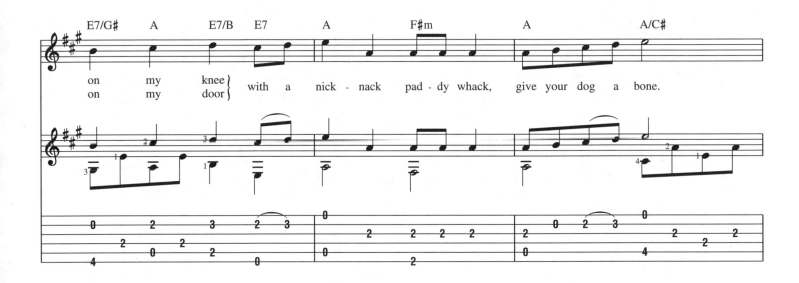

on my knee}
on my door} with a nick - nack pad - dy whack, give your dog a bone.

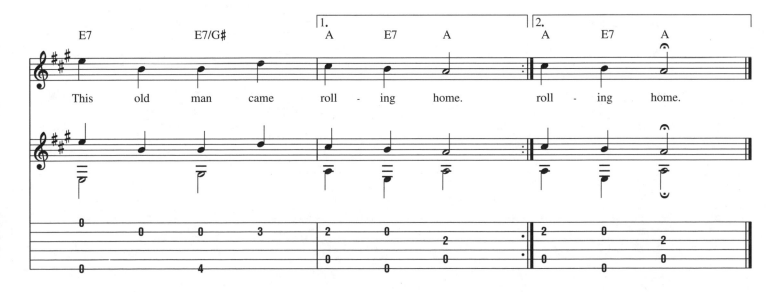

This old man came roll - ing home. roll - ing home.

Yankee Doodle

Traditional

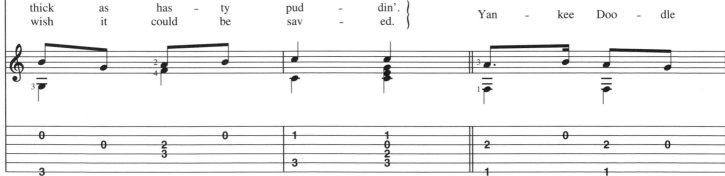

Additional Lyrics

3. And there was Captain Washington
   Upon a slapping stallion
   A-giving orders to his men,
   I guess there was a million.

4. And then the feathers on his hat,
   They looked so very fine, ah!
   I wanted peskily to get
   To give to my Jemima.

5. And there I see a swamping gun,
   Large as a log of maple,
   Upon a mighty little cart,
   A load for fathers cattle.

6. And ev'ry time they fired it off,
   It took a horn of powder.
   It made a noise like father's gun,
   Only a nation louder.

7. An' there I see a little keg,
   Its head all made of leather.
   They knocked upon't with little sticks
   To call the folks together.

8. And Cap'n Davis had a gun,
   He kind o'clapt his hand on't
   And stuck a crooked stabbing-iron
   Upon the little end on't.

9. The troopers, too, would gallop up
   And fire right in ours faces.
   It scared me almost half to death
   To see them run such races.

10. It scared me so I hooked it off,
    Nor stopped, as I remember,
    Nor turned about till I got home,
    Locked up in mother's chamber.

Take Me Out to the Ball Game

Words by Jack Norworth
Music by Albert von Tilzer

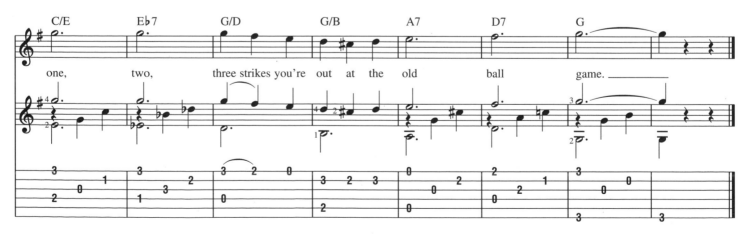